a poem is a house

linda ravenswood

a poem is a house
linda ravenswood

MADVILLE
PUBLISHING
LAKE DALLAS, TEXAS

FIRST EDITION

Requests for permission to reprint or reuse material from this work
should be sent to:

Permissions
Madville Publishing
PO Box 358
Lake Dallas, TX 75065

Cover art and design: linda ravenswood

ISBN: 9781956440652 paperback, 9781956440669 ebook
Library of Congress Control Number: 2023943087

Land Acknowledgment
linda ravenswood

i acknowledge that my home
& birthplace in California
exists upon the occupied territory
of hundreds of Indigenous tribes.
This homeplace has been stewarded by our Indigenous ancestors
since time immemorial.

i acknowledge the Gabrielino & Tongva peoples
as the traditional stewards of Tovaangar (the unceded territory of Los
Angeles).

i acknowledge the land & the water.
i acknowledge that tribal continuity
& community preservation depends on clean, shared,
secure & sustainable land & water access.

i acknowledge the history upon which the state of California has been built,
how policies, systems & structures of spoken & unspoken racism
oppress & erase People of Color.

i honor & respect the history
of the original inhabitants & places that preceded the founding of Los Angeles
& i am committed to sharing this history in my work.

i am committed to continuing the work
of kinship, listening, support & reparation as well
as building long-lasting relationships with Indigenous & other community partners.

i am grateful to work for the taraaxotam (Indigenous peoples)
& for their continuing flourishing, security & safety.

i offer thanks & homage to our shared Honuukvetam (Ancestors), elders,
& 'Eyoohiinkem (our relatives/relations) past, present & on their way.

table of contents

Foreword

In this, her latest, most formally inventive book yet, Linda Ravenswood, the Poet of Los Angeles, troubles languages and identities, rubs her back along salt spines, and eats your grandmother's pudding.

Russian symbolist Anna Akhmatova said poetry boils down to gossip and metaphysics—well, here is Ravenswood's gossip: the history of the *conquista* of the New World, the history of California, her white mother, her Mexican father (here enters metaphysics), her essential being-ness and between-ness, a mooring to and violent severing from history that compels the reader to ask: How are *we* continuous? How am *I* new?

Languages play across this book—English, Spanish, Nahuatl—with and without translation, echoes of a place unmoored from time. I'm reminded of Lars von Trier's film *Dogtown*, in which an empty set means there are no walls between neighbors except those in their minds. "To live at the scene of an accident" is a mantra/poem that cycles through this book—we are all at the scene of the accidents of our lineages and histories, the subtly shifting repetition seems to say. Likewise, what a poem fundamentally *is* shifts from section to section, with each section presaged by visual poems ("A poem is…a footnote/slave/woman" reads one) laying out a new thesis of poetry to set the palimpsest for (and create a meditation on) what comes next. In a vast and sprawling book, these repetitions give us a lens to look through, a song, and a sense of motion—a map, Ravenswood might say, or a compass.

Read this book when you're in your feelings, to zoom you out and remind you that you are history, embodied, a living tapestry of everyone who ever was and all they said and forgot and cherished. And wonder how the severed goat's head in the tree still sings—a reminder of what cannot be explained—even with all that history, cruelty, and beauty.

—Brian Sonia Wallace,
West Hollywood City Poet Laureate
Academy of American Poets

To live at the scene of an accident

To go on living
at the scene of a crime.

The children turn themselves into   *ICE*

Are you ice   **I am a flag**

I can be quiet

         I could pretend
you never existed   & the walk across
the desert a dream. I could imagine
your rig an ice cream truck
your siren   the song that calls me
to the street.   I can imagine the desert
is a street.   this border jag the way
to school.   this fence a fence between
two grand properties. my father the king
of the mountain & land to the west.
my uncle of the domain beyond.
there are orchards & olive trees
& peaches. fishponds of my mother
in a diaphanous dress. I can imagine
it's a movie, my pockets full of corn.

I heard a little girl on the opposite side
of the *Rio Grande* successfully turned
herself into ice & floated downstream.
she was that kind of glacial child who
tripped a little   left a little   & flowed.
when she finally came to the sluice gate
en La Paz it was just enough to scoop
out of the water. there was just enough
story left

remember everything but be quiet
as stone. imagine stone.
be the kind of book
that holds oblivion.
if you can be that quiet.
if you can be that useful.
if you can be that slate gray

pequeña Joanna Semilla de manzana
turn yourself into ice.

2

a poem is a history genocide city

To live at the scene of an accident

To walk by a vast park
where I played as a child
& be oblivious to play.

To drive by iron gates
where my hand
was crushed in imperial hinges
& not be jolted.

To go on living
by the scene of a crime.

To bake bread there,
cut grass, hang out laundry.
To have counted days
since a catastrophic event
only to be caught in a breezeway
holding fresh apples, realizing
it's spring. To wander
to the other side of grief, vacantly.
To fidget, to be mild.
To sigh in the silence of moderation.
To forgo fanfare or cataclysmic surges. Even briefly.
To dwell. To be simple
in rain. Turning home.

a poem is a house floating on water

**names of Malinche / names of her children / no such thing
as half-breed / only new celestinas**

They call her complicated—
Ichpochtli Cihuatl Ko'Olelo X-ch'uupal tongue *la lengua*
interpreter wife concubine spy peacemaker pacifier map maker collaborator
translator messenger captive-girl woman *nahua* slave indigenous chattel
Grijalva Xicalanga Yucateca princessa—sing it
Grijalva Xicalanga Yucateca princessa! Grijalva Xicalanga Yucateca princessa!
Our mother.
   —See her son Martín
   clutching her like a peat-colored horseshoe
   a lap dog prickly pear *un hijo de pitaya roja*
   see his claws & wooden limbs
   see what burden is the new star—
   crumbling & cracking everything around him
   everyone running *is it flood is it locusts*
   no one stopping to see his dew // his eyes.
   everyone afraid of the ingression—the power of the nascent explosion.
   a new city on a hill sends mudslides below—
   land bursts to new civilizations covering a beautiful plaza.
   See Martín in his mother's clutch
   how they interpret his face like an alien,
   not new beauty on the mountain.
   See how his father paces back-and-forth in the hallway *is it my son maybe*
   it's not my son (is it my son!?) maybe it's the son of the water or the waves is it
   even a sun maybe it's a girl there's a boat in the harbor I can get home if I hurry
   I never knew them anyway was it a son or a Cacahuate I'm allergic to
   este flores nativos get me out of here what is it a Sun anyway

Is it Indigenous. Is it Spanglish. don't say *Pocha* they forget us in the West.
Beyond the border / *Mexica mestiza* /
Hijas de latinidad / *Aquí* / There is no half-earth
Madre tierra / *hija de Nepantla* /
Don't turn us away / *Sus Hijas immaculatas*
**There's no such thing as a half-breed human
look a new star on your tongue**

poem. **grandmother book.** *el libro de la tatarabuelita*

page 1
like a star
billowing in the oven.
her tin foil

        page 2
        her potatoes with salt   *papas con sal*

page 3
freshly scrubbed snow monkeys
huddled on wallpaper—
she picked them
instead of orchids

        page 4
        evenings
        she'd switch on the record player.
        it whirred warm & low
        like another animal in the house

page 5
in sunlight
she drove us   *white Chevy Monte Carlo*
places we belonged

        page 6
        on her lap
        an ice nest &
        cold bowl of sweet pudding
        (cherries jubilee is delicious)

page 7
one summer
outside Hesperia
she looked
through the car window—

some places remind me of things
does that happen to you …

when daddy got arrested
he thrashed so hard
in the cop car
they sent a bill to mama
for damages.
it arrived
to the funeral parlor
& followed us
every place we moved
for years.

i don't think we
ever did pay it

page 8
springtime was
her tin
of butter cookies   *biscochitos con canela y azúcar*

page 9
she showed us
days in green grass
& somehow lives
in all good
green things
wherever we go   *en todo bien*

To live at the scene of an accident

To be oblivious to play

> but go on living

> at the scene of a crime.

a poem is a woman ^{footnote} ^{slave}

footnote
slave
a poem is a woman

Mixpantli—Malinche

Es una *historia de Malinche* no ficción creativa o antropología o poesía o mitología o
eventos actuales—ai no—siéntate mija, déjame contarte todo

(Is *a Malinche story* creative nonfiction or anthropology or poetry or mythology or current
events—ay no—take a load off, lemme tell you everything)

When first you came you were great grey *y* blue
a fresh robin egg you had
liquid stickem stick him victim &
inside pink & red & eyes that bulged like globes of water recalled you daughter
reached for me said *do what you must.*
so you started to look like this *y* look like that
lengthened your tibia in the tradition of girls sent from one region
y boys for one thing or another *luchar por la'escuela y ser un hombre //*
in the tradition of girls to potatoes *y* boys who become trees *y* rockslides
y aqui—Malinche—the burnt one baulking on the promontory
sets out
wind in her hair
throws her *tilma* on her neck
signing the ancient spiritual   *sometimes I feel like a motherless child*
á veces me siento como'un niña sin madre
huehuecauhtica yolaactihuetzi calpanpilli
huecauh yenepa huecauhtica
chan chan ichan yenelli tlaneltocaqui

I link arms with you   link arms across time with you /
the women's building covered in graffiti no woman drew
the women's building covered in graffiti no woman I know drew
the women's building covered in detritus thrown by someone who doesn't like women //
who shant think of women the way they think of men or houses or dogs or rubles
& yet the women's building is tended on wknds by a man who pushes a broom for the cause
so praise women-respecting-men who tend our townhall & call it progress
these trans auto-ethnographic experiments trance across hypertext transfer juxtaposition
translate images *pero como vas a pagar la gasolina*

her book was just published she's won the Rome prize no one can hurt her
she's sailed across waters & white women—several well-meaning white women with white-women hands
worked in suds *y* maybelline / be like them learn from them watch out for their purse *y* sugar nothing can

hurt her she's home in Manhattan her book just published she goes to meet her husband at the puck building she's flown through the window of her Manhattan apartment through the delicatessen awning below her play just closed on Broadway her movie's in the can *she said something to me I didn't like actually it wasn't me I was in Fla. at the time she was mean or no I wanted to steal things but she came back in & saw me so I had to kill her* he hangs her on her own shower fixture but the dust from the renovation next door cannot conceal the truth she's won the Rome prize she's in her Manhattan apartment she's flying through the window he says *somehow my wife the artist has flown through the window it's true we argued but somehow she has learned to fly* I link arms with you link arms across time with you across gender the Korean American trans boy who never ordered any woman around loves *tacos* but doesn't grok Chicanx culture just yet but it's *tacos y kimchi* he'd never brandish a shiv he loves *sopes y Hoeddeok* the *molcajete* is his mother / Alan Nakagawa crosses out his mistakes they become part of the literature / for a cis man there is no mess it's art & madness / acceptability trailing like an untethered relative a woman must be perfect *sin cicatrice* no cicatrice no cicada on the Record *tsk tsk tsk* no blur I link arms with you Marsha *mi madre* Marsha P Johnson my mother rises in roses the pier at Christopher street wakens with your perfect singing your perfect body you turn dock water to roses

pause & retreat if mother sends me out I will find a way a farrow I will come up clean
so the green spring rises from the sleepy grain I will parry with semiots & liguisters / douse
& dance they'll call me inauthentic *pocha* haters will look slantways & I
will slough them *como los cascabeles que son y* I will weather with men in helmets *y*
bayonets / will find the green beret & glove & boot & call home the artists &
murdered wmn   I will carry my sister home use language my shield & buckler no
man will know me save my body & plum   I will draw followers & confound the
unimaginative   they will call me a walnut but realize I am a sword
my pronunciation *y* Beckett mouth will move them
some will call me serial killer some will call me *Tia*

we shall be *le vide sans pareil* / started with a walnut kept its body pristine /
like a splayed squid in the desert *y* wrapped in edible gold / the chorus of Saint Martin in the Fields
will sing over it with breath—dry it slowly with humility—add shattered olive oil &
seasoned pink salt *y pimiento*—a virginal girl from Udaipur will encase it
in the *au jus* of cleansed basil leaves—oh what is this recipe you make on shin &
terrace overlooking Coatzacoalcos—who comes for your feast days &
where did you go when you were little—where did you hide—
on your tricycle *y canoa y acalli*
Come out girl   come out   ven ven ven   *ben ben ben*
a tu casa
a tu hogar ancestral
a tus tierras ancestrales

To live at the scene of an accident

To wander
to the other side of grief

a poem is **war**

My fathers eyes in the sloe time gravity of kelp beds off Baja California Sur

& Papa I love you
& do not regret places we never ran
you were with me on the courts in Los Feliz
over glyphs & the Mulholland swank down.
you draped across dunes.
there is no knot in my language
when I see the places you dwelt

& Papa I love you
your eyes are closed like Georgia O'Keeffe shell number two.
my breath on you
the feather whisper
wondering if you're in Burbank
or in the cloud
of a child
in some other portico

> *by the plaster Maria say 10 Marias*
> *12 Marias   18 Marias*
> *for my father gone down to the place of shells,*
> *y agua y green things swaying*

even in the bracken Papa I love you
your eyes are the dust of *La Ribera*
where the ancestors bent & fished
by *La Salina* I love you
for things you did
knowingly unknowingly intrinsically
in your DNA I love the blood & bones of you
& the remnants of you
in your cashmere
under the earth.

you kept goats & now
you are kept by them
on your hill

y Papá recuerda la cabeza de cabra
cortado pero cantando en los árboles
— fue el viento escalando a través
de cada lugar donde estás es un carnero y una cabra
donde sea que estés, el cordero y la oveja se acuestan en la tierra
ai Papá no me arrepiento de haber tocado apenas tu mano antes de que te fueras*

* & Papa remember the goats head
severed but singing in the trees
—was it wind climbing through
every where you are is a ram & a goat
every where you are is the lamb & the sheep bed-down in earth
oh Papa I have no regrets that I barely touched your hand before you were away

a poem is a memory housefire family

To live at the scene of an accident

To not be jolted.

To go on living
at the scene of a crime.

an aetiology of wings on a whyt laytee
or metaphor for the borderland
in the voice of the mother of Malinzin

I came home to find I'd forgotten to let the ghost out
the whole length of summer
       it was dead, of course
       crouching like an iron skillet to the floor
a snug door stop
some mother purse
       Get rid of it I blazed in the mirror
       even as one was in the throes
of doing just that.
Holding it at handletail
       I watched it
       being marshaled to the bins
one always forgets something when one leaves home
one day one'll come it'll all be burnt

a poem is gold
gold
gold
gold

the dream of the grass blowing

it's the dream of the grass blowing & someone says
there are Damson pears we dance in pairs a thin woman
with the world air-raid around because she's thin *y* able a horse
in clothes rides along her wind-on-the-arm-of-the-world
she says *here are pears take them if you want*
but we're off to Portland where grass can blow along the Willamette
going out to meet the day no time to waste for water or women

Untitled note from Oregon

after Jana Harris

A pair of bloodstained gloves in tall grass was left. A sigil. From Winesap
into the Columbia. That was the place where they slept
somehow unbothered by fleas & ticks. Grass went high
as a horse head & even the donkey lay down.
On the lower ridge they pulled mosquitoes to their fists
10 or 15 at a time. Boils on their necks & in dark places
oozed for months. The babies sucked rags dipped in the blood of offal
but came through winter.
                                        On bluffs overlooking the Okanogan
we saw native women coming with Camas hanging from their belts.
They placed the bulbs in a pit & covered them over with sweet grass.
When the Camas had steamed they sliced them like onion heads.
A sweet purple taste. Smokiness of earth & seeping greens.
With translucent Camas tongues falling on our fingers
we looked to the sky, straining to find a bridge
from our grandparents & saw
they had left us everything.

a poem is a disappearance

the carriage ride / with my whites / 7 generations out

once I was a child she climbed
            the mountain in Los Feliz.
said *king of the mountain*
            & I knew it was my turn.
said
            against the small of my back.
this will all be yours
            don't worry
don't worry
            I rode my bicycle all on her spine
don't worry she said
            it doesn't hurt
it's only the family business.
            we bridled up with the horses
& drove out to Pasadena
            along the Arroyo
the wind was whistling
            through her good ear
& down her clavicle.
            her teeth were rattling
& she said
            don't worry it's fine
we looked at each other
            in the backseat
eyes following us
            cauling us
she said
            it takes a long time
to know how to own the land.

house
dance
history
flight
song
burden
bed
door

a poem is a

Receipt

You need this poem
This poem is a Compass
You will never be lost
if you have this poem

I bring you a receipt
from my ancestors
& the movies
to remind you
everyone loves the flaming yellow gorse
they never tire
hearing about it
(What I once thought was repetition
is essential)

This poem is a receipt
who will I be to you in 5000 years
keep this receipt / you will know /
Ynez. Stella. All the people in the boat
The great cloth of heaven
diamond dollops between black stretches.
this. what names can tell. & time.

y Now
the cabman is Irish
he presses the traffic like a river fish
knows his way around the *Plaza*
Alvarado looks like the detritus
of a turned over carnival
burned beachfront
black underbelly of the works
in axle grease & sweet wrappers.

The *Rio Grande* was once the border.
Now every cement block-cum-zip-code

is new territory
how will we tell the story
of how much brilliance *y* confusion
lives in the west.
What is a trailhead, Grandma?

They came / borders were crossed.
Erase it.
Some said white is as white does.
Then, even she disappeared.

Mexicans came running to dry
the tears. Mexicans always
dry the tears of weeping children
in the West. Warm milk. *Nopal* on eggs.
Oh to be a Mexican woman
when children cry
baking bread in the warmth of cotton dresses
& the flesh of their embrace.

Pull the stops for the widows & orphans
make a casserole
send heaviest pots *y* fresh fruit
transgress
Dance with the ghosts of land & sky.
Come home. Transgress, Come home. Remember
you are Americans.

Driving to the theatre
Now
The cabman is Moroccan.
He understands the road
Hold the receipt
This poem is the receipt
I am American / Something of a bloviator /
else I would keep these prayers to myself
But being American & from the West
I sew these to your pocket as well

Remember / This poem is a Compass /
You will never be lost
if you have this poem.
Throw your eyes on the sky.
Even your enemies will rend the edges of their shirts
when they hear you've gone from the world
into the midst of your fathers
Know this name from the West //
in the great tremble
of Invented Americans
some dreams come
on long legs
with short memories

Ode to America

oh electric guitar
& black banjo
oh sounding man on a homestead   man with fists in dirt

                    & coming down

        a woman

                with curtains in her hair

        behind black &   snowshoes & garbled gravestones
        white & red   sucker punch
        & brown trailing   & grin & bear it

all the way to work
some contract creaking yesterday

    & more   there will be more   amen

aunt susie

search   search to search
for the lost aunt
aunt who never was

aunt on a barstool. in her classroom. aunt driving solo in her car.
side slick glances in her click round everywhere mirror. her clutch visor check
for guys on the backstreet a lip slant brush for liptricks & mirror flips of lipstick ticks
on the lip tip of her white & mint green cigarette. lipstick El Lay ley lines & school
teacher mauve lipstick for 1970s *y* 1980s boyfriends when things were good for an
LAUSD lip trip primer donna with lipstick hands, lipstick car, lipstick gas tank lit on
fire *y* let that Pinto roar down LA Streets *donde* Mexicanos come running *con*
hose-wares, to put that beast out its conflagration *y* knock it out of booze trouble so
crack that fire on Cahuenga near the children in grief she sits grinding her math
problems *y* glue into Mexican children banging erasers in the asphalt sun   hey aunt susie
I'm circling the perimeter *aunt Soosie* I call up the institution windows *you in there*
send down your lipstick kisses your whole lipstick Rapunzel chains aunt Susie send
down your deep aerosol lipstick eyes your deep iconic yellow hair *y* lipstick fingernails
y magenta lipstick trigger finger on your gun *en Mar Vista* way down to that lipstick
dog you said was your best loved being of earth

a poem is a   diaspora

in the sky which is called history

crossing sand   map in mouth
un perro con agrupador   there's lightning in
windows   in a sky
  country called history.   mexican
pilgrims walk. across   the desert
       eyes belting
their way by Joshua trees.
their song
a steady breath

a hush
a yawn
a click   to the future

but here
  a sheriff   has arrived   ahead
of the caravan

he   pours   drinking
water   onto   the
ground

    left out   for   the
travelers   in   agony

mud puzzle   holy chain of life
whispering   whispering away
in red dust

no   psalm   or
dance of thanksgiving
                 he says

someone has littered the desert again

a pretty
deputy   sails   the   empties
two at a time
        into the police truck.
        her   khaki arm   loops & swells
        over
          itself   a löie fuller of silt.
something   to scrawl   home
        about.

            scribes—
ping down your reportage like stars.
witness
these   red
marrowbones
on frames
bending for centuries.   *como
las estrellas*
how they chew themselves awake.

it was written
*they would wander a lipsline of
history*
a quiet rattle   their family
name

To live at the scene of a crime

To be crushed
by imperial hinges
but go on living.
At the scene of a crime.

Suitcases

They arrived. Naugahyde & polyurethane
suitcases covered in cake & dish towels.
Airline tags. Luggage octopi coiling the road off jetliners.
They rolled-up carrying the beaches of Tel Aviv in their hair.
Burned things in the kitchen,
split hotdogs on the grill & under each move
bellowed how everything they did was correct.
(it was). They rolled with cooking sets & seltzer bottles
ugly clothes & worse sandals
showing us how to be Jews in America.
They never slept, soaked in the jacuzzi,
stayed in, played cards like for diamond antis,
drove relatives cars like evolving off the side of the universe,
smoked in the bathtub, knew every one of our dirty magazines,
slipped us money and marzipan, kept coming through seasons.
Snug gatherings of some-of-them would recede
& other branches would rise.
The survivors. They'd already almost died
so not one of our remnant had time to be sick but
bulldozed with everything bright ahead
& we dialed up Fairfax & the Black Sea Restaurant,
Canter's Deli & Schwartz Bakery
& no one was on pills, just a little sensitive to noise
fingering wee, European, saccharine-capsules
like the heads of pins
to keep things bitter sweet & sane.
Every once in a while
they'd talk about how much money
they'd had before the war, but
consoled themselves with The State Of Israel,
Mount Carmel in the sun,
wonderful buses, ice cream
& girls with machine guns.
Everywhere the armed youth

off the Dizengoff slit their eyes to every corner,
& the remnant felt safe. Finally.
This was before we moved to Century City
& before other groups of them came & left
& came again & went home
& disagreed with my parents
& never came back
& made up & came again
then never again,
& it went in cycles of yes & no
on transatlantic wires
under oceans in dark dreams
then into the light.

Until they all disappeared
like precious fog. Vanished
singing their stories
& we almost pictured them
in Valhalla.

It was long ago
& even I wonder
was that me or them
or did I read it in a book,
was it part of a dream
what was that time
between the 6 days war & pandemic
that used-to-be-time
open time, time of learning
soft kirsch cheese & Nikon cameras,
airplane bags of history.
What were those days he cried
in his gabardine
oh you were the last,

...were you the last!?

after Daniel Borzutzky, The Book of Non-Writing

nothing bodies words

They fly. All the bodies. walking trouser legs. sweet swirl in the streets.
They rust. like engines. bodies so old they go over & again lumbering with big bellies
& fat hands. trees shut up from dirt. crashing over. bodies thrown of land. bodies in the
field. they rope on. everywhere a vast landscape. their nuts & bolts. the leavings &
comings & goings of the body in it its spray. in itches & folds. the smell. like leaves
turned over like something rained on. weight aching & long in its mind & muscles.
the body taken over by screaming by laughter by crying the body taken over by love.
the idea of love. the mirror indication of love. the deck of cards way a button shines.
through an eye. in a shirt. a shirt song by the body for the body. the only slightly
imagined end of the body. the very definitive edge of the body. the smell of the body.
again. the smell of the body. the body through the nose of grass. the smell of the body
in ice. the smell of bread in the body. the smell of the body after it's been covered in
bread. bread that makes the body the bread of the body. the longing for the body of
bread.

the body without borders. *sin fronteras*. the body with no borderland no edges.
the body as a spooled out plane. the body as the plane itself. the body the field.
the body the entire earth. the body without the boot in the basement. without the green
hat in the silt the body without trouble. the body without wine without the goats head
hanging from trees the body without rope. without twine. the body without levers.
the body from under the body. beyond its own blood & sinew. the body beyond
taxation. beyond representation. beyond immolation. beyond self satisfaction.
beyond putrefaction. the body beyond the body.

the body in a cave. the body in a glass of water. the body in a space capsule. the body
in the moon. the body in the space between the moon & the earth. the body floating
to the dark side of the moon. the body explaining the dark side of the moon to a child in
its new body. the body understanding that it cannot know everything about everybody.
the body in the picture show. the body in theatre chairs every weekend. the body
holding a newspaper in its clutches. the body never ending eating. never ending
swimming. never ending bathing. never ending trying on shoes. the body never ending
spinning. singing. mapping. writing. the body never ending calling up poems of the
body aloud before a grand body within the body of a house within the body of a city
within the body of the earth. the body never being without the earths body. the body
and the earths body traversing traveling marrying living kissing cooking fucking yelling

dancing. the body the body the body the body the body until forever the body until the light changes the body until the car doors slam the body until we say good night the body beyond until the body beyond reframed the body beyond death the body beyond loneliness the body beyond loneliness the body beyond loneliness the body beyond motherhood the body beyond the doorman the body beyond the marketplace the body beyond the body the body beyond need the body

this is not really a lullaby for the end of the world this is a map to the beginning of the body. the body on the lip of the volcano. the body and its wedding gown. the body laughing because it is a judge. the body laughing because it is a prostitute. the body knowing laughing because it is a merchant and if you sold a precious earthly bauble to a body in need as it increases its savings as it dances with its goals the body as it dreams of future images of itself in future rooms antique chests & vaults & beds & tables elevating itself rocking itself to sleep the body as it dreams of never ending the body smelling its fingers for evidence everybody saying it's too hard to make a movie let me be a writer & let spells be enough everybody needs a script for this is not really a lullaby for the end of the world this is the beginning of the body

apples turn.

                       before apples turn
      they blink.   & smudge.
      sweet soft turns.
                   a man's arm   as he ages.
sweeter. softer.
             cider for breakfast.
a little longer.
turn for vinegar.

         at the window   a man.
                           (who neglected to cry.
                           who forgot to cry.

                           who set store
                           by other dailies.)
the way
a bent man   throws hot food   around his mouth.
spectacles. & clouds.
looking to see   what's come   of his apples.
shakes his glasses to see.

what is the end of apples   for a man who cannot cry

ghost
stranger
friend
a poem is a husband

Elementary school

for Brigit Pegeen Kelly

there was a goats head hanging by ropes in a tree she said.

you have to forgive men
I immediately wanted to say for how long.
I knew she'd say it's a process and a cycle
that we have to thank them for wheels and the trips to CVS and the houses
that it's a balancing act for everything everywhere
that marriage is about — in the end — coming to an agreement
that you both need each other especially as you get on in life.
Three husbands, four husbands, lots of sons.

The song of the night bird she said.

they say it's something men are
like it's what boys do
something comes over them
maybe it's a little bit biology maybe it's a little bit dark anatomy
they just don't know why they did it
they were in a group of them and it was like a cloud
they all saw red or black or some color
it's built into society to forgive them
to punish them hard and then forgive them
to punish them hard and never forgive them
it's built-in you have to say sorry and you have to mean it

cried like a man and struggled hard she said.

even a woman recognizes the struggles of a man
even a woman talking about murderous intent of children

who happen to be young men in the making
even there a sweet song of forgiveness shocks the night with its beauty
and tenderness   the sweetness of I'm sorry
everybody cries for a man
the man you lost
the man you never knew
and would you be surprised to know
your own father had a dungeon
not a metaphorical dungeon
but a dungeon where he did things that men do
things he needs to be forgiven for
things he will be forgiven for
songs he'll sing to be forgiven for
the way his song goes on forever
when his song is cry for forgiveness
for the things men do

To live at the scene of an accident

To go on living at the scene of a crime.

on divers memorias

1

> from
> the
> tree
> of
> life

2

> the mendieta
> figure emerges
>
> ripping herself
> out of the tree
> out of the backdrop
>
> (she was there the whole time)
>
> the tree becomes the building
> becomes the sky
> y everyone is flowers

3

> someday everything will be flowers
> but today there is a diversity of species
> the mirror drops so Close
> we jump across a subtle plane
>
> everyday

4

> Can you see
> the brown person
> at the edge of a white woman's gaze
> like a continent
> like a hammer

5

> Ramiro makes pictures
> of elite houses
> across Los Angeles
> y never removes the brown cook
>   brown leaf blower
>   brown nanny
>   brown gardener
> from the frame
> those workers
> spend more time
> in the mansions
> than the white people
> who own the places
> in the end
> a bus ride home
> far from the beach

6

Steadfast as an immigrant on the waves
swallowing leagues of salt water
or cactus heel'd in the desert

there's a man
coming out of the landscape
his arm above his head

stop the train
a man is coming

100,000 bells of my heart ring
will there be land

7

I know what it's like to be the brown person
at the edge of a white woman's gaze because
my mother is the whitest woman in Los
Angeles / Mayflower descendant / in my
bedroom / I'm making forts *y* tents on the
floor with my lacey duvet // *get off the*
floor // dirty indian // you can take the dirty
indian // out the landscape // but you can't
take the dirty Indian
out the dirty indian /

inter-familial racial trauma
is a piece of glass under the tongue
& endless
to be the brown child
in a house of *gringos*

8

we never talk
about racism at home
just what we see on tv

a poem is iron
iron
iron
iron

1519 water dream

Chontales people on the cliffs of Yucatan
see Cortés' ships approaching, north of Tlapaco.
They imagine the structures might be unknown houses
hovering, floating towards land.
Perhaps land itself imagines—
Perhaps animals wonder.

1

It's 1519.
I'm a Bird.

    (I with my I)

see with my eye
say with my eye

it comes to
rest on the desert—

a house
coming
on water—

a piece—
missing of its own tongue

2

look—
   a chunk
    on water—
flowing—
following—

stalking—

     frontera
     drags
along the bottom

   jettisons the ocean
as it slides

look now—

a piece

boiling on the water

                     tell all   your friends

3
a House-on-water

4   I'm home

I'm a bird   *who holds the paper here*
I know this desert   *ask that bunch of Indios over there*
 a falcon   *who holds the title*
  returning home   *andale, lo mismo*
  a bird turning   *I see ... a hotel—*
it cannot be all bad   do you see it ...
a bird must turn in the desert
to give birth to many brothers

& apple trees

5   *Imagine it*

what new language
  plastic in the throat
  of water birds.   it's 1519
                                 i am a bird

                  some evolution—

a poem is a choir
choir
choir
choir
choir

anyone who saw me might've thought I was dancing

—Lot's wife

1

anyone who saw me might've thought I was dancing
might've thought I was railing

my cloak round me breaking
free from the underbrush, light

of the city behind me
spinning, our temples on fire.

our golden bowls.   were they
laughing or screaming or crying or singing.

anyone who saw me
might've thought I was dancing

might've thought I was raging,
flicking a flea from my forearm;

an animal, a hare, a roadsnake,
(anything met in nature is frightening.

& winds
anything that creeps deeper than you is frightening.)

if anyone'd seen me they'd've thought I was dancing
or turning for story, a kiss. maybe.

if they'd seen me rolling
they'd've thought I was racing

a leaf. a rock. (many times
we turn to show what's been gathered.)

2

if they saw me in moonlight
(imagine the night

was clear
after the meleé

clouds low enough
that trees could be moved by them

nudged, would have spilled
round the horizon)

my form like new laundry
like a geyser developing

jolted awake.
if I'd been a pillar of salt

some deer could've stroked
its tongue on me

some moose or antler bearer
some small ruffian of the fields

an otter or prairie dog.
I wonder if that's how the pillar'll come down

not like ozymandias in
an aajej but like the song

of a whole village
laid out on one woman's voice.

3

I met a man on the road, a man who could hear. He was confused but
pointed to the river, beyond the mountain. I was lugging my baby, wasn't
sure what to do, lay down, pitch a tent, throw rocks, yell all night. I thought
he might be good so against the wind & the Bracken I listened while he said,
in the night, by the spring, with the crickets, he was a man who could hear.
somehow, my better judgment from past men, the teachers, my cousins,
my brothers, even all of the women, through all empirical data, something
biblical, believed him, wanted to believe, wanted to go on where he was
turned, in the desert, alive.

To live at the scene of an accident

    To be crushed
    by imperial hinges
    and not be jolted.

To wander
to the other side of grief

To go on living
even at the scene of a crime.

Acknowledgments

In addition to winning the 2022 Arthur Smith Prize, *a poem is a house* was first finalist for the Rachel Wetzsteon Prize from *MAP* and the Gunpowder Prize from *Alta*. Additionally, several poems from the collection won individual prizes: the 2022–2023 Oxford Prize in Poetry for "Elementary school," and the 2023 Edwin Markham Prize in Poetry for "The children turn themselves into *ICE*."

Poems from this book have appeared in the following publications:

Cantadora: Letters from California: "1519 water dream" (Eyewear Publishing/ The Black Spring Press Group)
Fireweed: Poetry of Oregon: "grandmother book"
Gulf Stream Magazine: "to live at the scene of an accident"
Oxford Poetry: "Elementary school" (Partus Press, for The University of Oxford, The Oxford Prize, 2022)
Reed Magazine: "The children turn themselves into *ICE*"
Variant Literature: "untitled note from Oregon"

I should like to thank editors Linda Parsons and Kimberly Davis at Madville Publishing.

About the Author

Linda Ravenswood BFA MA, PhD abd is a poet and performance artist from Los Angeles. Accolades include an Oxford Prize in Poetry (2022) and the Edwin Markham Prize in Poetry (2023). She is the founding editor of *The Los Angeles Press*, est. 2018, and the co-founder of the Poet Laureate program in Glendale, California. Recent collections include *Cantadora— letters from California* (Eyewear London/The Black Spring Press Group, 2023), *The Stan Poems* (Pedestrian Press, 2022), *Tlacuilx—Tongues in Quarantine* (HINCHAS Press, 2021), and *XLA Poets* (HINCHAS Press, 2020). Find her at thelosangelespress.com

www.ingramcontent.com/pod-product-compliance
Lightning Source LLC
Chambersburg PA
CBHW022030080426
42733CB00007B/790